WALLINGFORD PUBLIC LIBRARY
WALLINGFORD, CONNECTICUT 06492

Japanese

ART & CULTURE

Kamini Khanduri

Raintree

Chicago, Illinois

WALLINGFORD PUBLIC LIBRARY
WALLINGFORD, CONNECTICUT 06492

J709.52
KHA

© 2004 Raintree
Published by Raintree, a division of Reed Elsevier, Inc.
Chicago, Illinois
Customer Service: 888-363-4266
Visit our website at www.raintreelibrary.com

All rights reserved. No part of this book may be reproduced or transmitted in any form or by any means, electronic or mechanical, including photocopying, recording, taping, or any information storage and retrieval system, without permission in writing from the publisher.

Printed and bound in China by South China Printing Company

07 06 05 04 03
10 9 8 7 6 5 4 3 2 1

Library of Congress Cataloging-in-Publication Data:

Khanduri, Kamini.
  Japanese art and culture / Kamini Khanduri.
      p. cm. -- (World art and culture)
Includes bibliographical references and index.
  ISBN 0-7398-6609-5 (library binding)
  1. Art, Japanese--Juvenile literature. 2.
Japan--Civilization--Juvenile literature. [1. Art, Japanese. 2.
Japan--Civilization.] I. Title. II. Series.
  N7350.K42 2004
  709′.52--dc21
                            2003001957

Acknowledgments
The publishers would like to thank the following for permission to reproduce photographs:
P. 5 Oriental Art Museum Genoa/Dagli Orti/Art Archive; pp. 6, 41, 49 Michael Yamashita/Corbis; p. 7 Michael Freeman/Corbis; p. 9 Gunshots/Art Archive; p. 10 Bettman/Corbis; pp. 11, 15, 48 Burnstein Collection/Corbis; pp. 12, 27, 29, 43, 45 Sakamoto Photo Research Library/Corbis; p. 13 Private Collection/Sally Chappell/Art Archive; pp. 16, 18 Christies/Corbis; p. 17 Claude Debussy Centre St Germain en Laye/Dagli Orti/Art Archive; p. 19 Impact Images; p. 20 Kimball Art Museum/Corbis; pp. 21, 34, 35, 36, 40, 50 Archivo Iconografico, S.A./Corbis; p. 22 royalty free/Corbis; pp. 23, 33 Seattle Art Museum/Corbis; p. 25 Kozu Collection/Kyoto/Werner Forman Archive; p. 28 Frank Leather/Eye Ubiquitious/Corbis; p. 30 Takashi Yamaguchi/Pacific Press; p. 31 The Royal Cornwall Museum/Bridgeman Art Library; p. 37 Dallas and John Heaton/Corbis; p. 38 Paul Seheult/Eye Ubiquitous/Corbis; p. 39 Ric Ergenbright/Corbis; p. 46 Fukuhama Inc./Corbis; p. 47 Corbis; p. 51 The Kobal Collection.

Cover photograph of a Meiji period lacquered Noh mask: Honeychurch Antiques Ltd./Corbis;
Cover photograph of a Nishijin brocade: Nicole Irving.

Every effort has been made to contact copyright holders of any material reproduced in this book. Any omissions will be rectified in subsequent printings if notice is given to the publishers.

Content Consultant:
The publishers would like to thank Anne E. Guernsey Allen, Associate Professor of Fine Arts at Indiana University Southesast, New Albany, Indiana, for her assistance with this book.

Some words appear in bold, **like this.** You can find out what they mean by looking in the glossary.

Contents

Introduction

Japan is a long, narrow country situated on the western edge of the Pacific Ocean. It is made up of four main islands—Hokkaido, Honshu, Kyushu, and Shikoku—and several smaller islands. Because the north of Japan lies near Russia and the southern islands stretch beyond South Korea, the country has a wide range of weather conditions, ranging from snowy winters to subtropical summers. Located on a **plate boundary,** the mountainous landscape is interrupted by volcanoes and frequent earthquakes.

Japan is slightly smaller than the state of California. Nearly 75 percent of its land is mountainous and uninhabited, and about 15 percent is used for agriculture, mainly rice-growing. This leaves only about 10 percent of the land for people to inhabit. That is not very much,

considering that almost 127 million people live in Japan—a little less than half the population of the United States.

Japan is often described as a country of contrasts—old and new, quiet and noisy, empty and full. In the big cities, such as the capital, Tokyo, life on the streets is hectic and fast-moving, with flashing neon signs at night and busy shops and restaurants on every corner. Yet life indoors is quite different, with an emphasis on calmness, politeness, uncluttered space, and simplicity. Japan can be seen as a land of skyscrapers, crowds, and fast trains, but also of ancient temples, poetry, and **tea ceremonies.** Its people have seen major industrial developments since the 1960s, especially in areas such as computers, electronics, and cars. While Western influence is obvious, Japan has not lost a connection with its own traditional values.

This map of Japan shows the great distance between the northern tip of Hokkaido and the southern islands as well as the mountains that leave much of Japan undeveloped.

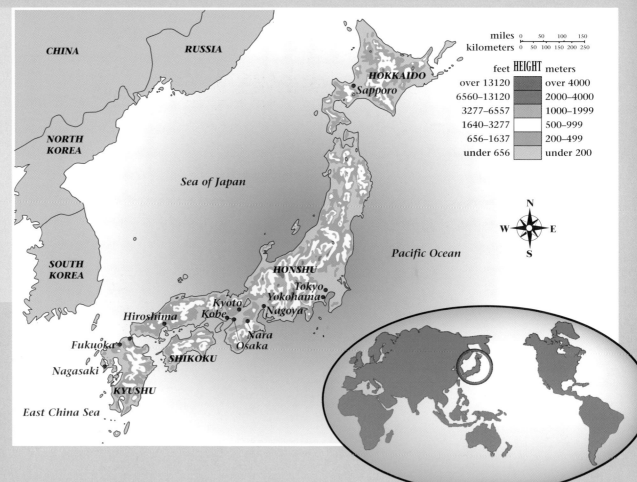

miles 0 50 100 150
kilometers 0 50 100 150 200 250

feet	**HEIGHT**	meters
over 13120		over 4000
6560–13120		2000–4000
3277–6557		1000–1999
1640–3277		500–999
656–1637		200–499
under 656		under 200

CHINA

RUSSIA

HOKKAIDO
Sapporo

NORTH KOREA

Sea of Japan

SOUTH KOREA

Pacific Ocean

HONSHU
Tokyo
Yokohama
Kyoto
Kobe
Nagoya
Hiroshima
Nara
Osaka
Fukuoka
SHIKOKU
Nagasaki
KYUSHU

East China Sea

N
W   E
S

4

Paper and silk

Two of the most commonly used materials in Japanese art are paper and silk. Paper is used for paintings, prints, and **calligraphy**; on the walls and windows of tea houses; for paper-folding called *origami*; for kites; and for puppets. Paper-making is a craft in itself, and paper can be plain or decorated, white or colored, in one piece or layered in a collage.

Silk is used for painting and calligraphy and in armor, clothes, and theater costumes. Textile design is an important art form, and in the **Edo period,** well-known artists were often commissioned to design patterned **kimonos** for dancers and other famous women.

This print by Chobunsai Eishi (1756–1829) depicts a woman wearing a beautiful silk kimono.

Japanese art

Japanese art reveals a great deal about Japanese culture. Although influenced at various times by China, Korea, and the West, the arts and crafts of Japan retain a strong identity of their own.

Japanese artists generally attach great importance to the natural materials they use to create their art. They are not overly concerned with achieving a "perfect finish." In fact, they sometimes aim at a level of imperfection and roughness; being able to see the potter's fingerprints on a finished pot might add to its artistic value. There is also an appreciation of irregularity, or **asymmetry.** For example, Japanese poetry is written in verses of three or five lines, rather than in pairs, which is the usual form in Chinese and Western poetry.

In Japanese art, empty space is as important as filled space. The focus is on understatement rather than overstatement (on less rather than more) and the bare essentials. This **minimalist** approach can be seen in Japanese art forms such as dry landscape gardens, **Noh** stage sets, and **interior design.**

Inspired by nature

Japanese people have a great respect for nature, and nature has been inspiring Japanese art since the first paintings were produced there. The ink landscape paintings of the 15th century, the ornate screens boldly painted with plants and animals, the hugely popular landscape prints of the artists Hokusai and Hiroshige—all these take nature as their theme. Many aspects of nature can be seen in Japanese art, from the seasons, different types of weather, and favorite scenic spots to trees in blossom, mountains, rivers, and the sea. Many kinds of plants and animals, including cranes, frogs, and tigers, are also included.

Cherry blossom

The cherry blossom is an important part of Japanese culture and has always been a popular subject matter for artists. People all over Japan gather in large groups to view cherry blossoms on trees in spring. The blossom is beautiful but often lasts only a few days before being blown away by the wind. It is just this short existence and fragility that gives it its great appeal. An 18th-century poem written in the form called **haiku** captures the sentiment:

Once again in love
once again regrets, fleeting
as cherry blossoms.

Picnicking under cherry trees is a popular springtime activity in Japan. People bring food and drink and enjoy the beauty of the blossoms.

c. 10,500 B.C.E. to 300 B.C.E., **Jomon:** Time of prehistoric hunter-gatherers, then early agriculture. Clay pots and figures.

c. 300 B.C.E. to 300 C.E., **Yayoi:** Large-scale rice cultivation. Clay pots. First bronzework.

c. 300–552, **Kofun:** Time of early emperors and huge tombs. Clay tomb figures called *haniwa.* Shinto shrines.

This 19th-century woodblock print shows a samurai warrior wearing armor and wielding his sword.

1603–1868, **Edo:** Peaceful age. Capital moves to Edo (today called Tokyo) and Japan is closed to the outside world. The arts flourish, including woodblock prints, **netsuke,** porcelain, **Kabuki** theater, and **Bunraku** puppet theater.

1868–present-day, **Modern:** Japan opens to the outside world and becomes an industrialized nation. Western-style and traditional arts coexist.

Painting

Japanese painting was greatly influenced by the work of Chinese artists. The earliest paintings had a **Buddhist** theme and were displayed in temples along with Buddhist statues. Gradually, a native Japanese style of painting developed, with nature, particularly landscapes, as its main subject matter. This Japanese style was called *yamato-e*.

The most widely used format was the scroll. Both horizontal handscrolls and vertical hanging scrolls were used. Hanging scrolls were hung on the wall as pictures. Looking at a handscroll was more like looking at a book: you put it on a table and unrolled just so much of it at a time as you could comfortably hold between your two arms—a section of about 16–20 inches (40–50 centimeters). Some handscrolls, called **narrative** handscrolls, contained writing as well as paintings. In these, the pictures and the words together told a story.

◈ Paints and brushes

Paintings were done on paper or silk, using a brush to apply inks or watercolors. Like **calligraphy** brushes, brushes for painting were made from the hairs of animals such as badgers, rabbits, sheep, foxes, or even mice. Brushes came in various shapes and sizes, depending on the type of painting they would be used for. Black inks were made from wood soot, and colors were made from minerals such as malachite (green), lapis lazuli (blue), iron (brown), or other natural materials such as crushed shells (white). These were mixed with glue to make the paints.

This amusing scene, from the late 12th-century handscroll known as *The Frolicking Animals*, shows a frog and a rabbit having a wrestling match while other frogs watch in amusement.

10

Winter Landscape by Sesshu Toyo is a fine example of his dramatic presentation of Zen landscapes. This ink painting was completed in the 15th century.

Zen paintings

During the **Muromachi period, Zen Buddhism,** a form of Buddhism emphasizing meditation and intuition, greatly influenced painting. Many major temples set up studios, and some monks became artists. They painted scrolls, screens, and sliding door panels for display in palaces, wealthy people's houses, and even in temples. Most of the paintings the monks produced were landscapes done in black ink.

The best known of the Zen landscape painters was Sesshu Toyo, the son of a **samurai.** He entered a monastery at age eleven and was ordained a Zen priest a few years later. He studied ink painting in Kyoto, then set up a studio in southern Japan. In his late forties, he spent two years in China, and the paintings he saw there influenced his work. Sesshu is known for his stark, dramatic pictures and his use of angular lines.

◈ Rolling scrolls

Both handscrolls and hanging scrolls could be rolled up. Before rolling a scroll, the artist had to make sure the paint was fully absorbed by the paper or silk, because a layer of paint left on the surface would flake off during rolling. Since rolled scrolls did not take up much space, even people with small houses could keep collections of pictures, bringing them out for display on special occasions. Valuable scrolls could also be easily rolled up and taken to a safe place in the event of calamities such as wars and earthquakes.

Painting on a large scale

Large paintings on surfaces such as sliding doors and folding screens had been used to decorate people's houses since **Heian** times. From the **Momoyama period** onward, the styles became more extravagant, with rich colors and gold decoration. Subjects included all aspects of nature, ranging from flowers, trees, and birds to dramatic paintings of animals such as tigers and hawks.

Screens and doors were often used to decorate the splendid castles that were built during this period, since the dark rooms with small windows were considerably brightened by the paintings. As a display of authority, people in powerful positions hired the best-known painters of the time to decorate the interiors of their castles and palaces in an incredibly lavish style.

Folding screens

Folding screens became popular among ordinary people because they were both works of art and practical items for daily use. They are still used today. Screens are freestanding and can be placed anywhere in a room, and so they might be used to create a background or to divide the room into different areas. Traditionally, screens are always used in pairs.

Ogata Korin

Ogata Korin, the son of a textile merchant, was probably the greatest of the screen painters. Even today, two of his paintings, *Irises* and *Red and White Plum Blossom*, are among the best-known paintings in Japan. Korin took nature as his subject matter, created a simple, strong design, and painted it onto the surface. The bold designs appealed to rich Edo merchants, who were Korin's typical customers.

Part of Ogata Korin's 18th-century pair of painted screens, *Irises*, celebrates the beauty of nature, a constant theme in Japanese art.

Decorated fans

The Japanese invented the folding fan, which is made of paper or silk and painted with ink or watercolors. The fan's sticks are made of wood, such as bamboo, and are often **lacquered.** Because of its shape the fan provides one of the most interesting formats available to the Japanese artist. Fans are used in everyday life, for keeping cool, and just for decoration. They are also the most important accessory for **Noh** actors.

This late 19th-century English fan is an example of how Japanese art influenced Western arts after the country opened to international trade in 1868.

Sliding doors

Japanese houses were, and still are, open plan. Sliding wooden door panels, made by carpenters and furniture makers, are used to create separate rooms. They operate in pairs—in fours, in sixes, or even in eights. To open a pair of doors, you slide one behind the other; with six, four, or eight doors, you open the two central doors symmetrically. Sometimes a room might be surrounded on all four sides by painted panels.

The panels are covered in paper, which is then decorated. Artists painting on sliding doors have to remember that not all the panels will always be visible, meaning that each panel has to look good on its own, as well as when forming a part of the whole painting. Sometimes, artists divided up the painting in a particularly interesting way. For example, in Nagasawa Rosetsu's 1787 painting, *Bounding Tiger,* the only thing painted on the door on the far left is the tip of the tiger's whiskers!

Woodblock Prints

During the second half of the 17th century, Japanese artists started producing woodblock prints. These were pictures created by printing ink onto paper using blocks of wood. Early prints were made from black outline blocks and colored in by hand until about 1765, when color prints appeared. When these woodblock prints were introduced to Europe and the United States in the 19th century, they became the most popular form of Japanese art in the Western world and went on to influence many Western artists.

The floating world

At about the time the first prints were being made, a new style of Japanese painting was emerging. Known as *ukiyo-e*, which literally means "pictures of the floating world," the style showed popular activities such as music, sports, and theater treated in a realistic manner. The *ukiyo-e* style was quickly taken up by the printmakers, who made it their own, taking the actors, wrestlers, and beautiful women of the time as their main subjects. The "floating world" refers to the fleeting nature of life and to the philosophy of enjoying its brief pleasures.

Ukiyo-e developed to satisfy the taste of a wide range of people, but in particular that of the merchant classes, many of whom had become wealthy. It also appealed to the **samurai,** who, with time on their hands now that the civil wars had ended, were looking for new pastimes. These people enjoyed the entertainment districts that were growing up in the cities.

Art for all

Unlike paintings, woodblock prints were cheap to make because they could be **mass-produced**—the same blocks could be used to make any number of prints, meaning the prints were often cheap to buy. Prices varied, depending on size and quality, but in the mid–19th century a print cost roughly the same as a bowl of noodles (a meal for most ordinary people). So, unlike earlier types of Japanese art, woodblock prints were just as likely to be found displayed in a peasant's cottage as in a wealthy samurai's house. There was great demand for these affordable souvenirs of everyday life, and the more pictures were sold, the more were produced. The publishers who commissioned and sold the prints responded energetically to the public demand.

◈ How prints were made

Making color prints required the skills of a team of craftspeople. First, the artist drew an outline design, and then an engraver cut this design onto a block. Next, the printer made a number of proofs from this block, and then the artist painted each proof with a different color: red parts on one proof, blue on another, and so on. Using these proofs as a guide, the engraver cut the color blocks, one block for each color. The printer applied the colors to the blocks and then printed each block onto the paper to make up the picture. Artists today use the same technique to make woodblock prints.

信ほるの儀といふべかりける

悩をうりて出るを主とふんことを

Suzuki Harunobu was one of the first artists to produce color woodblock prints like this one, called *Truth-Sincerity*, in the 18th century.

15

Actor prints

Many prints featured the celebrities of the time: the **Kabuki** actors. These actors were famous much like the sumo wrestlers and beautiful women of the day, and audiences wanted portraits of them dressed in costume. Since photography had not yet been invented and most people could not afford to commission paintings, prints were a more affordable option. Prints announcing particular performances or portraying an actor in a certain role functioned like movie posters do today.

A return to landscapes

By the early 1800s, travel within Japan had become more common, particularly among city dwellers going on trips to the country or the coast. Publishers began marketing woodblock prints to tourists as souvenirs of their journeys, and the subject matter began to change to cater to this new audience. Prints of well-known landmarks became popular, paving the way for the landscape prints of Hokusai and his successor, Hiroshige. The direction of printmaking thus turned back to its traditional subject matter.

Katsushika Hokusai was one of the most talented and influential of all the print designers. He created thousands of prints as well as paintings and book illustrations. He is best known for his series of striking landscape prints, *Thirty-Six Views of Mount Fuji*, which made him famous in his own lifetime.

Mystery man

Amazingly, the artist Toshusai Sharaku produced all his work (about 140 actor prints) over a period of only ten months between 1794 and 1795. While earlier artists had treated their subjects as heroes, Sharaku's portraits of the Kabuki actors are powerful, dramatic caricatures full of humor, irony, and even cruelty. Sharaku's life is something of a mystery, but there are many theories—for example, that he was, in fact, another artist using a different name, or that he was an actor himself. His prints may well have offended actors and their fans, a good reason for him to paint under another name.

Sharaku's style is easily recognizable. This print is entitled *The Actors Nakamura Konozo and Nakajima Wadaemon in Character*.

Views of Mount Fuji

The print known as *The Great Wave,* from the series depicting Mount Fuji, is probably Hokusai's best-known piece of work. The dramatic composition of a huge toppling wave in the foreground, with Mount Fuji tiny in the background, is possibly the most famous Japanese image in the world. Japanese people were, and still are, fascinated by Mount Fuji, and it is a popular theme in poetry and art. Fuji has always been considered a sacred **Shinto** site; even today, climbing it is seen as a religious pilgrimage. By depicting Fuji many times, Hokusai reflected public awareness of the mountain as a magnificent yet dangerous landmark. When Hokusai was alive Fuji had not erupted for over 50 years, but residents of nearby Edo (Tokyo) were well aware that it was an active volcano and held it in due respect.

The Great Wave by Hokusai is also called *Mount Fuji Across the Water,* or *Fuji Seen through the Waves off Kanagawa.* It is one of the series *Thirty-Six Views of Mount Fuji* and was created in 1834–1835.

This print showing a windy day at the 44th station on the Tokaido road is typical of Hiroshige's gently humorous style.

◇ Hokusai on Hokusai

Hokusai was a slow starter, and, at the age of 75, said of himself:

"...of all I drew prior to the age of 70 there is truly nothing of any great note.

At the age of 73 I finally came to understand somewhat the nature of birds, animals, insects, fishes.

... Therefore at 80 I shall have made great progress, at 90 I shall have penetrated even further the deeper meaning of things, and at one hundred I shall have become truly marvelous..."

(Hokusai, translated by Richard Lane)

In fact, Hokusai died at the age of 88.

The Tokaido road

Like Hokusai, Ando Hiroshige became famous for his landscape prints. His style, though, is gentler and less dramatic. Hiroshige is best known for his series *Fifty-Three Stations on the Tokaido Road*, which was so popular that thousands of copies of the prints were made. So many were printed that the wooden blocks completely wore out and had to be recarved.

The Tokaido road ran between Edo and the old capital of Kyoto. It was frequented by people from all walks of life. Fifty-three lodging stops, or stations, were built along the road so travelers could stop for food, a change of horses, or a night's sleep. Hiroshige's prints were used as souvenirs, as records of travel, or even as the equivalent of postcards to give to friends and relatives.

Hiroshige shows the various features of the landscape along the road as well as the changing seasons, the different times of day, and the weather conditions. He also shows the activities of people, such as farmers, craftsmen, merchants, and travelers, some of whom are using the road, others of whom live near it. One theme running through all the prints is Hiroshige's gentle sense of humor.

Sculpture

Sculpture is one of Japan's oldest arts. Over the centuries, a wide range of materials has been used by sculptors: clay, bronze, wood, stone, and dry **lacquer** have been carefully crafted into all kinds of objects. But Japan is probably best known for its many and varied **Buddhist** sculptures.

Early sculpture

The earliest Japanese sculptures were clay figures made during the prehistoric **Jomon period.** The figures often look like people or animals but are also strangely abstract. No one knows what their purpose was, though people have suggested they were dolls for children or images of gods and goddesses.

Looking at sculpture

Unlike painting, sculpture is a three-dimensional art. To really appreciate a clay figure or a Buddhist statue, you need to touch the object, feeling its shape and the texture of the material from which it is made. When you look at Japanese sculpture in a museum, you are not usually allowed to touch it, but it may be displayed so that you can see all of its sides—for example, in the middle of a room, rather than positioned against a wall.

Visitors to the Daibutsu (Great Buddha) at Kamakura are able to walk around the huge sculpture and view it from every angle.

Keeping guard

More than 5,000 years after the first clay figures, during the **Kofun period,** large numbers of hollow clay sculptures called *haniwa* were made. At this time, royal or **noble** people were buried in enormous tombs and the *haniwa* were placed on top of the grave mounds. They had tube-shaped bases so they could be pushed into the ground. It was common practice in many early cultures to bury pottery objects with the dead, but *haniwa* are unusual in that, instead of being buried in tombs, they remained outside. Their purpose was probably to guard the tomb and to protect and watch over the dead.

Boats, animals, humans, and houses

The earliest *haniwa* were just simple cylinders, but then human figures and, later, birds and animals were made. The human figures were often carved with amazingly detailed costumes, and they represent people from all walks of life, including **falconers,** farmers, soldiers in armor, priestesses, and ladies of the court. There are even musicians and dancers posing as if in mid-performance. Sculptures of houses were also made to represent the home of the dead person's soul, and boats symbolized the transportation of the soul to its resting place. The *haniwa* figures give us a fascinating insight into the society that created them.

On this *haniwa* of a horse, the detailed carving of the saddle and bridle are clearly visible.

In Sanjusangendo in Kyoto, there are 1,001 gilded statues of Kannon, goddess of mercy. They were commissioned in 1164 and were carved by a team of 70 craftsmen.

The arrival of Buddhism

The introduction of **Buddhism** to Japan in the 6th century was very important for the development of Japanese sculpture. Demand grew for statues that served as objects for people to worship in the many temples that were springing up all over the country. There were statues of the Buddha himself, of other holy beings (called *bodhisattvas*), of famous Buddhist monks, and of disciples of the Buddha known as *rakan*. The figures ranged in size from tiny to gigantic, and the styles changed over the years as different sects of Buddhism, such as **Pure Land** and **Zen,** were introduced and became popular.

Bronze, stone, clay, and **lacquer** were all used for Buddhist sculpture, but by the **Heian period** most sculptures were made of wood. This was probably because of traditionally held beliefs: it was thought that trees were the sacred homes of spirits, which made them particularly suitable for sculpting objects with spiritual significance.

◈ Sculpting wood

Early Heian statues were made from a single piece of wood, except for the arms, which were sculpted separately and then fitted into the rest of the body. In the 11th century the famous sculptor Jocho perfected the joined-wood technique, in which each section was carved from a different piece of wood, then joined together. This needed more planning but allowed the sculptor more artistic freedom.

The Kamakura Buddha

The statue generally known as the Kamakura Buddha is one of the most enormous Buddhist images in the world. This bronze statue with a calm, serene expression on its face stands approximately 40 feet (12 meters) high. The upper part of its body, including the head, chest, and shoulders, is bigger than it should be (given the proportions of the lower part) because the huge image was designed to be looked up at by people standing on the ground a long way below. The Kamakura Buddha was cast in separate horizontal sections, which were then joined together to form one huge image. Workers scraped around the joins with metal files to make the lines less obvious. Today, the statue stands exactly where it always has, but the wooden temple that once enclosed it was swept away by a tidal wave in 1495.

◈ Zen Buddhism

Monks returning from China introduced **Zen Buddhism** to Japan during the **Kamakura period.** The principle of Zen is that you can achieve enlightenment by living a simple life close to nature and by practicing meditation. Zen Buddhism inspired many of the arts, in particular landscape painting, **calligraphy,** pottery, and garden design.

The Great Buddha at Kamakura in Kanagawa Prefecture was sculpted from bronze in the 13th century.

22

Later sculpture

During the **Muromachi period,** Zen Buddhism grew in popularity and began to have more influence on the culture of the time. Zen Buddhism inspired many varied art forms, but the creation of sculpture gradually became less important. Demand for the furnishing of new temples ebbed away and the golden age of Buddhist sculpture, which had lasted for almost 1,000 years, was over. Some statues were produced in later years, but many sculptors moved toward carving different objects such as masks for traditional **Noh** plays and **netsuke** (see below).

Netsuke

Traditional Japanese clothing consisted of a robe worn with a sash around the waist. There were no pockets, so people used to attach things like purses or tobacco pouches to a cord, slip the cord through their sash, then attach a little toggle to the other end of the cord to keep it in place. These little toggles were miniature sculptures called netsuke. Netsuke became popular among the merchant classes during the **Edo period** and were mostly made of wood or ivory.

Carving netsuke was quite a challenge because they were so small and yet had to function as practical items. Over the years they got smaller and smaller—some were only about 1 inch (less than 3 centimeters) high—and yet the carving was still extraordinarily detailed. In the second half of the 19th century, as Western clothes began to replace traditional robes and sashes, netsuke were no longer useful, and carvers moved back to producing larger objects.

Carved characters

Netsuke carvers drew their inspiration from a wide range of subject matter, including animals, mythical creatures, gods and goddesses, and the world of entertainment. Dancers, actors, and sumo wrestlers were also favorite netsuke subjects. Sumo wrestling, which had once been practiced at local shrines and temples, became a professional sport in Edo in the mid-18th century and was as popular then as it still is today in Japan. The best wrestlers became as famous as the great **Kabuki** actors, and prints of them, both fighting and off duty, were produced for their supporters.

A netsuke made of ivory called *Hotei and his Treasure Bag.* Hotei was one of the "seven gods of good fortune." He was the god of happiness and of children, and he is usually shown with a large stomach and a bag.

Metalwork

The art of metalwork came to Japan from China in the **Yayoi period,** when bronze and iron were used to make early weapons, coins, mirrors, bells, and ornaments. With the arrival of **Buddhism** came bronze statues. Later, when the **tea ceremony** became popular, large numbers of cast-iron tea kettles were crafted. But Japanese metalworkers are probably best known for the swords and armor made from the **Heian period** onward. Although the primary purpose of these objects was either ceremonial or military, they were also seen as outstanding works of art.

Swords and swordsmiths

Traditional Japanese sword blades are curved and made of steel or a mixture of steel and iron. **Hilts** and **scabbards** are usually made of wood, but are often decorated with metal and **lacquer.** Swords come in different lengths, including long *tachi* swords, which hang from the waist pointing down, and short *wakizashi* swords, which are thrust through the belt pointing up.

In the Heian period, swords were worn by **nobles** for ceremonial purposes. From the **Kamakura period,** with the change to a warrior culture, they became important as weapons for the **samurai.** Stronger, lighter, and sharper swords that were more efficient in battle were made. The samurai visited **Shinto** shrines, where they prayed for victory, offered gifts, and gave thanks after success in battle. This spiritual connection, together with the high social status of the samurai warriors, meant that great significance was attached to their swords. Swords were considered sacred objects, and sword-makers, called swordsmiths, began to be treated in an almost religious way. They wore white clothes, like Shinto priests, and carried out purification rituals before making a new blade. Each sword was believed to have its own spiritual life, and success or failure in battle was attributed to the spirit in the sword.

◇ How blades were made

The swordsmith made, or forged, a blade by heating it in a very hot furnace while beating it into shape and repeatedly folding the layers of metal. A blade could be made up of 10,000 extremely fine layers of steel. When the blade was finished, the smith put it in the fire again, then cooled it in water. This process, known as tempering, was performed to harden the metal and caused patterns of wavy lines to appear on the surface. Often the smith would engrave his signature or an inscription onto the blade, after which he would polish it.

Armor styles

Japanese armor was always decorative as well as practical. Styles changed according to the battle techniques of the time—for example, whether soldiers were on foot or on horseback.

From the 10th century, a style known as *o-yoroi* was worn. This consisted of a lot of plates of iron and leather joined together in rows by brightly colored silk cord and then heavily lacquered for extra strength. Soldiers also wore iron helmets, often with horns on the top. *O-yoroi* was rather bulky and did not fit the body very closely, so by the 14th century it had been replaced by lighter and simpler styles. Then when guns were introduced in the 16th century, styles changed again, with armor plates getting larger and helmets getting stronger.

In the 17th century, when the age of battles was over, armor became more decorative and less practical. Ultimately, it was just a symbol of a samurai's wealth, and often it became so ornate it would have been useless in a battle!

This exquisite set of 16th-century samurai armor, including a fearsome helmet, was actually made for a child.

For hundreds of years, most Japanese pottery took the form of pots or jars, rather than plates or bowls. The pottery was used for storage or cooking rather than for serving food and drink, since most wealthier people ate and drank from **lacquer** bowls, while ordinary people tended to use wooden bowls or plates. In the 16th century, with the arrival of the **tea ceremony,** pottery bowls were used for drinking tea, but it was not until the 17th century that pottery plates and dishes were used regularly for serving food.

Early pottery

The first Japanese pots were made 12,000 years ago in the **Jomon period.** Large and cone-shaped, they were mostly used for storing seeds and grains and for cooking. Jomon foods would have included wild plants, nuts, fish, seafood, and many types of meat. When Jomon people later began growing crops such as beans, a wider range of pots developed. There is evidence of such variety that it has been suggested that each family made its own pottery using its own designs.

Changing tastes

During the 6th and 7th centuries, Japan was greatly influenced by the cultures of China and Korea. A wider range of shapes, new types of decoration, and more advanced pottery techniques, such as colored glazes, were all introduced to Japanese potters. As with many other art forms, potters adapted the new ideas to create their own Japanese style.

In 1185 the **Heian period,** in which an **emperor** had ruled over a court of **nobles,** came to an end. Instead, a military government was set up with warrior leaders. Tastes in pottery changed, too. Plainer pots replaced the decorative pieces that had become popular. This development was influenced by the warriors' more practical tastes and by the simplicity of **Zen Buddhism,** which had been introduced by then. One typical shape from this era is a narrow-mouthed jar called a *tsubo* that was used for storing seeds.

◈ Art or craft?

In Western cultures, a distinction is often made between a piece of art that is on display, such as a painting or a piece of sculpture, and an object that has been crafted for everyday use, such as a pottery jar used for storing seeds. In Japan both are equally admired. Whereas Western artists tend to focus on the end result, to a Japanese potter, the clay used to make the pot and the way in which it is hardened in the fire are at least as important as final effects such as surface decoration.

A Jomon period clay pot has a decorated rim and a cord-marked surface pattern.

Cord-marked pots

Jomon pots were usually made by piling coils of clay on top of each other. Sometimes the coils were smoothed together, and sometimes they were left visibly separate. A piece of rope or cord was then wrapped around a stick and pressed or rolled onto the still-damp surface of the clay to make patterns. This is where the name of the period comes from—Jomon means "cord-marked." Some later pots had extraordinary decorations added to their rims, including geometric patterns and shapes resembling human or animal faces.

The arrival of tea

Tea came to Japan from China at the end of the 12th century and was originally only drunk in temples as a kind of medicine. In the 15th century, Zen priests held the first **tea ceremonies** in grand rooms and used expensive Chinese pottery.

It was the 16th century tea master Sen no Rikyu who developed the simple, intimate tea ceremony that was so popular during the 16th and 17th centuries and remains an important part of Japanese culture today. Rikyu stripped the ceremony down to its bare essentials and emphasized simplicity. The only equipment he used was an iron kettle, a plain container for the tea, a bamboo tea scoop and tea whisk, and rough black tea bowls, known as *raku* ware (see opposite).

The tea ceremony

The tea ceremony is a traditional ritual for entertaining guests. Influenced by **Zen Buddhism,** it is intended as an escape from the cares of the world. A formal tea ceremony today lasts up to four hours. First, the guests wait in a quiet part of the garden, where they wash their hands in a stone basin or a pebbly pool. They enter the tea house by crouching through a low doorway. The host serves a meal, then thick tea, followed by thin tea. The guests all drink from the same bowl to show equality. Although translated into English as the "tea ceremony," the Japanese phrase *"cha no yu"* actually means "hot water for tea."

A traditionally dressed host prepares tea for her guests in a contemporary tea ceremony.

Pottery styles

The tea ceremony had an enormous influence on the production of Japanese pottery and the development of styles. Many kilns were set up where items including tea jars, tea bowls, tea caddies, and water containers were made for use in the ceremonies. Simple, rustic, rough shapes were popular, both glazed and unglazed, decorated and undecorated. In addition to *raku* ware, other types of pottery were made at different kilns, including cream or white-colored *Shino* ware, which was thickly glazed and often had simple designs, and rich, reddish-brown, unglazed *Bizen* ware. Although tea wares generally remained plain during the **Edo period,** pottery used for serving food was often more decorative.

◈ Firing clay

There are several different techniques for firing clay. Early pots were fired at low temperatures in open pits or ditches. These low-fired pots are called earthenware. Stronger pots fired at higher temperatures are known as stoneware. By medieval times pots were fired in kilns at high temperatures, and porcelain was fired at an even higher temperature. Potters can achieve a particular result by firing a pot in a certain way. For example, *raku* pottery is fired at a low temperature and taken out of the kiln while still hot, since it is the rapid cooling of the clay that creates the special color and texture of the surface.

Raku bowls

Raku tea bowls are plain and simple, with irregular shapes, glazes, and decoration. They are small enough to fit comfortably in the hand, which helps the user to feel the warmth of the tea through the pottery. They are made by hand, rather than on a wheel, which adds to the irregular finish. Most *raku* bowls have a small, round foot and almost straight sides. *Raku* ware is still very popular today.

This black *raku* ware tea bowl was made by Hon'ami Koetsu, who made many tea bowls. *Raku* tea bowls were so individual their makers often gave them names. This one is called Amagumo and dates from the early 17th century.

Porcelain

In the early 17th century, a Korean potter named Ri Sampei is said to have discovered a fine, soft, white clay in Arita, on the island of Kyushu in southern Japan. This type of clay had been used in China for many years to make a fine pottery called porcelain. Soon many types of porcelain ware were made at Arita, including the famous *Imari* wares. Colored porcelains, called polychrome, were made using bright green, yellow, and red pigments. The most popular type was white porcelain with blue decoration, known as blue-and-white.

Blue-and-white porcelain was first made in China and Korea, and the technique, introduced to Japan by Korean **immigrants,** quickly became very popular. All kinds of plates, dishes, and cups were made in a range of sizes and shapes including circles, ovals, rectangles, squares, and diamonds. The **mass-production** of blue-and-white porcelain helped lead to the widespread use of pottery for serving food and drink in Japan.

Dutch dishes

Korean and Chinese porcelain had been **exported** to Europe for many years and was very popular there. During the second half of the 17th century, China was involved in internal wars and was too busy for trade. The Dutch East India Company, which had a trading post in Nagasaki harbor in southern Japan, began exporting blue-and-white and polychrome Arita porcelain to Europe and Southeast Asia. This industry became very successful, and some of the porcelain produced was of a very high standard.

Porcelain produced at the Arita kilns, like this bowl, became very popular in the West.

30

This stoneware tea bowl was made about 1923 by Shoji Hamada. It is interesting to compare it to the tea wares of the 16th and 17th centuries, such as the *raku* bowl on page 29.

Folk pottery

As machine-made mass-produced goods spread all over the world, less and less handmade pottery was being produced in Japan. During the early part of the 20th century, the art form was barely alive. In 1925 the National Folk Arts Society was founded to try to address this decline in handicrafts. Led by Dr. Soetsu Yanagi, the Society supported small-scale potters working in all parts of the country and collected and displayed their work in museums. Yanagi's friend, Shoji Hamada, was one such potter, and his work has had great influence, both in Japan and elsewhere. Today, Japanese pottery is a thriving industry, with artists taking inspiration from their own traditions as well as from those of the West.

◈ Pretty on the plate

The presentation of food was, and still is, of great significance to the Japanese. The way the food looks on the plate is just as important as how it tastes. Foods of complementary colors and textures are put together to make the meal look as attractive as possible. The shape, size, and style of the plates or dishes is also given consideration. For example, rice or beans might be served in a small, rough, undecorated stoneware bowl, and fish on a large, smooth, rectangular, blue-and-white porcelain plate.

Lacquerware

Lacquer is a hard, waterproof substance that comes from the sap of the lacquer tree. It has been used in China and Japan to decorate wooden objects for hundreds of years. An early type of lacquer decoration was used in Japan from about 500 B.C.E., but it did not become a significant art form until after Chinese lacquering techniques were introduced in the 6th century C.E.

A coating of lacquer was initially used to make wooden objects waterproof, to stop them from rotting, to protect them from insects, and to make them last longer. Lacquer is also a good **insulator** of heat, so it was used as a coating for wooden soup bowls and other food containers. Over the years, the decorative aspect of lacquer became more important than its practical qualities. By the **Edo period,** the art of lacquering had reached a very high standard. Lacquerware was expensive and could only be afforded by the wealthy.

Traditionally, lacquer has been applied to wood, but it can also be used to coat basketry, leather, paper, and pottery. The art of lacquerware is very much alive today. Wood with lacquer decoration is still very popular, but the use of lacquer on plastic or metal surfaces is also common. Lacquered plastic is used to make all kinds of objects, including bowls, trays, lunchboxes, and chopsticks. Plastic bowls are sometimes decorated or colored to look as if they have a lacquer coating, even though they do not.

The lacquering process

Lacquering is a time-consuming and complicated process. A single object can take months to make. A number of different coats of lacquer are applied, and each has to be dried hard and polished before the next layer can be put on; several dozen coats might be used in total. Any decoration is added to the top layer. The process is made more difficult by the fact that unhardened lacquer is poisonous, so it has to be applied slowly and carefully.

The range of lacquer techniques includes flat lacquer, high-**relief** lacquer, and lacquer inlaid with gold, silver, or mother-of-pearl. Different regions of Japan use different techniques. Wajima lacquerware in Ishikawa Prefecture is most famous for the technique called *maki-e*, or gold-sprinkled decoration—probably the most characteristic of all Japanese lacquering techniques.

 **Maki-e**

Maki-e has been used in Japan since the 10th century. *Maki-e* literally means "sprinkled picture," because the technique involves sprinkling flecks of gold or silver onto the design painted on the top coat of lacquer while it is still wet. The metal flecks are sprinkled out of a bamboo tube, which has a screen acting like a sieve at its end. There are three main types of *maki-e*; the major difference between them is the way in which the design is polished.

Hon'ami Koetsu made this lacquered writing box in the early 17th century. He decorated the lid with cranes, a type of bird associated with the national identity of Japan.

Buddhas, boxes, and bowls

Lacquer was first used on **Buddhist** statues, and then it became the main type of decoration on things such as sword **scabbards** and boxes used for religious garments. Gradually it came to be used for a whole range of objects, including small items of furniture, decorative screens, combs, incense burners, theatrical masks, and **netsuke.** It was probably most widely used on boxes of all kinds: writing boxes, boxes in which to keep scrolls, tiny medicine boxes, and large chests used for storing **kimonos.** Lacquer was also used to coat everyday objects used by the wealthy, such as soup bowls and trays.

Architecture

The main types of traditional Japanese architecture are temples, **shrines,** castles, tea houses, and people's homes. In the past, houses were simple cottages or farmhouses with thatched roofs, unpainted walls, and undecorated wooden beams and pillars. The wealthy lived in splendid palaces and villas, some of which still stand today. Japan has plenty of forests, so wood was by far the most widely used material for building.

Today, concrete apartment buildings erected in the 1960s and brand new earthquake-proof skyscrapers stand alongside the temples and thatched-roofed houses of the past. In recent years many architects have taken inspiration from the styles of traditional buildings, while using modern technology and materials such as concrete and steel.

The first buildings

According to traditional **Shinto** beliefs, spirits or gods, called *kami*, were worshiped in the form of natural objects such as mountains and trees. Sacred places would be marked only by stone boundaries and piles of rocks, and no actual buildings were used for worship. Then, during the **Kofun period**, the custom developed of building temporary sacred buildings for the visitations of *kami* during festivals. Gradually the building of permanent shrines developed from this. Apart from the houses where people lived, these shrines were the earliest Japanese buildings. Shrines were made of wood and had thatched roofs, were usually raised above ground level, and were nearly always set among natural surroundings.

Elegant design

The Byodo-in temple near Kyoto was originally a palace owned by a **noble** Heian family. It was donated by them to be dedicated as a temple in 1053. The temple's most famous and only surviving building is known as the Phoenix Hall because of the bronze birds, called phoenixes, on its roof. Built on a small island in the middle of an artificial lake, the Phoenix Hall's elegant curves are reflected in the calm surface of the water.

The Temple of the Golden Pavilion (Kinkaku-ji) in Kyoto was converted from a villa to a temple in 1408. The current building is a replica, since the original was burnt down by an arsonist in 1950.

Buddhist temples

The arrival of **Buddhism** had a great influence on Japanese architecture. The first Buddhist temples, built during the **Asuka period,** were first modeled on Korean temples and later on Chinese temples, with their tiled roofs, red-**lacquered** pillars, and whitewashed walls. During the **Heian period,** temple architecture began to incorporate more native Japanese styles, such as wooden roofs and undecorated pillars. As different forms of Buddhism became popular, different styles of temple were developed, such as the **Pure Land** Buddhists' magnificent halls with attached gardens, or the multi-story temples of the **Zen** Buddhists, such as the Temple of the Golden Pavilion in Kyoto.

The main halls of temples, containing many Buddhist statues, were usually large buildings designed to hold many people for lectures, rituals, and services of all kinds, as well as for personal meditation. This organized form of worship was very different from the silent and individual interaction with spirits to which followers of Shinto were accustomed.

Holy pagodas

Early temples had a central tower called a **pagoda,** which was a separate building from the main temple hall. The pagoda was the holiest place in the temple because precious **Buddhist** objects were stored there. People were not allowed to enter the pagoda, but could walk around the outside of it while they worshiped. Later, halls and pagodas were given equal importance until, during the **Nara period,** the hall took on the more important role and pagodas became merely decorative structures.

The oldest skyscrapers

For many hundreds of years, temple pagodas were the tallest buildings in Japan. And yet, astonishingly, they have survived countless earthquakes when lower-rise, more recently built, and apparently more solidly constructed buildings have collapsed. Engineers have studied the techniques used for building the wooden pagodas and today use a similar method for constructing modern skyscrapers.

The 7th-century five-story pagoda at Horyu-ji Temple, near Nara. Nara, in central Japan, was the ancient capital city and has many fine examples of early architecture.

◈ Earthquakes

Japan's geographical position means it suffers from frequent earthquakes. This poses a constant challenge to architects. In 1923 the old city of Tokyo was reduced to rubble after a major earthquake. Much more recently, after the earthquake at Kobe in 1995, more than 5,000 people died, 35,000 were injured, and 300,000 lost their homes. One-hundred thousand buildings were destroyed and about 80,000 more were badly damaged. Many newer buildings stood firm.

Castles

Castles were basically military structures built for defense against enemies during periods of war. The oldest types of Japanese castles from the 7th century had earthen foundations and stone walls. In medieval times so-called mountain castles were built in many parts of the country and took advantage of the natural landscape of mountainous areas. In the late 16th century, many splendid castles were built. Guns were first being used during this time and so, to withstand these new weapons, castles were built with thick stone walls, huge stone ramparts, and moats.

Although built for military purposes, castles were also important in peacetime as symbols of a lord's power and authority. They were home to very large numbers of people: the lord, his family, his **samurai,** and his servants lived within the walls. Around the gates gathered the merchants and craftsmen, whose services the inhabitants used. In the immediately surrounding area, castle towns, known as *jokamachi,* grew up. Castle interiors were decorated with magnificent screens and sliding panels.

The White Heron

Himeji Castle is known as the Castle of the White Heron. It has white walls, elegant tiered roofs, and small windows. The castle is on five levels and has many turrets, gates, and walls. The main tower, or keep, is connected to the three smaller keeps by corridors. Himeji Castle was built for the **shogun** Hideyoshi in the late 16th century and was guarded by 3,000 samurai.

The famous 16th-century castle building at Himeji, southwest of Kyoto, is very popular with tourists, especially since it was featured in the James Bond movie *You Only Live Twice* (1967).

The tea ceremony's association with nature and simplicity is reflected in the quiet location of this unusual tea house, built on a lake and accessed by a bridge.

Tea houses

Tea houses are quiet places where the **tea ceremony** takes place. Sometimes they are called tea rooms or tea huts. The style they are built in is based on natural materials and simplicity, in keeping with the **Zen** principles of the tea ceremony itself. During the 15th century tea ceremonies took place in special rooms, but the 16th-century tea master Sen no Rikyu originated the design of the simple tea hut in 1582. Tea houses are usually found in gardens.

Most tea houses have clay walls, unpainted wooden beams, and roofs covered in rectangular wooden tiles, called shingles. Traditionally, the room should be four **tatami mats** (about 97 square feet, or 9 square meters) in area, and one enters by crawling through a low doorway. The windows are openings filled with a lattice of bamboo and fine white paper made from rice fiber, and sometimes the walls are covered with the same paper. Inside, the room is plainly decorated, with a hearth for the kettle, an ink painting or a piece of **calligraphy** displayed in an alcove, and a simple flower arrangement in the area used for meditation.

Gardens

Japanese people first created gardens around their houses as imitations of the sort of natural scenery found near sacred **Shinto shrines.** They were places for people to enjoy themselves or to spend quiet time, just as gardens are today. The earliest gardens appeared during the **Asuka period.** In the **Heian period,** gardens were often built around a central pond; water has since remained a key feature of many Japanese gardens. Other typical features are moss, bamboo, bridges, and paths of irregular stepping stones. It became popular to adapt the natural features of the landscape to create a garden, rather than trying to change the environment completely.

As **Buddhism** grew in popularity, gardens were attached to temples and monasteries as well as to people's houses. The **minimalist** influence of Zen Buddhism led to dry landscape gardens made of sand, stones, rocks, and raked pebbles. When the **tea ceremony** became popular in the **Momoyama period,** gardens were created with peaceful areas for tea houses. In the **Edo period,** wealthy **nobles** had beautiful landscaped gardens built around their palaces and villas. Gardens are still an important part of modern Japanese culture, and Japanese garden design has had much influence on Western garden tastes.

Katsura Rikyu

The Katsura Rikyu is a villa built near Kyoto in the 17th century as a country home for a noble family. Its garden is a splendid example of Japanese landscaping. The main building is surrounded by garden areas with groves of bamboo and several kinds of trees. From there, paths lead off to pavilions and tea houses. In the central garden is a large artificial pond with small islands in it and bridges across its narrower parts.

A view of the garden of the Katsura Rikyu from the inside of one of the pavilions. The sliding panels can be opened or closed.

Gardens as art

Gardens, unlike most other art forms, are alive. The living, growing elements that make up a garden are constantly changing with the seasons, the weather, the light, or just the passage of time. So, every time you look at it, the garden looks slightly different. A garden also needs regular care to keep it looking good.

Gardens have some qualities in common with other forms of art. They are entirely made up of natural materials, which are so important to Japanese artists, and are full of different colors and textures. Like a piece of sculpture or pottery, a garden is three-dimensional, but instead of just observing it from the outside you can go inside it, move around, and be completely surrounded by the work of art.

Rock garden

The Ryoan-ji is a **Zen Buddhist** temple that was built in the 15th century in Kyoto. It is famous for its dry landscape rock garden, which is filled with white river pebbles raked into various patterns. The novice monks at temples used to rake the gravel every morning as part of their training. Fifteen rocks of irregular shapes and sizes are arranged on the pebbles in five groups. It is thought that the rocks represent mountains, the pebbles represent the sea, and the whole represents a seascape in miniature. On three sides, the garden is bordered by a low mud wall and on the fourth side is a veranda. Unlike most gardens, you do not enter Ryoan-ji—you sit on the veranda and look at it.

An excellent example
of a bonsai tree.

The art of bonsai

Bonsai is the art of growing miniature trees in pots or trays. Bonsai trees are clipped
and given fewer nutrients so that they can never grow to full height. People keep
small bonsai trees in their houses and spend time looking after them just as they
would look after a garden if they had one. Today, many Japanese people live in
towns and cities where there is not much space, and so gardens are either small or
replaced by a porch area or an apartment balcony. Bonsai trees are a popular form
of small-scale gardening.

A room with a view

The link between indoors and outdoors is very
important in Japan. Both areas are seen as part of
the same overall space. Houses with gardens, such
as the Katsura Villa, often have sliding panels on
several outside walls that can be opened to reveal
the garden or closed to keep out the sun. A little
like putting different pictures on the wall, this
allows the people inside to choose which of the
different aspects of the garden to view depending
on the light, the weather, the seasons, or the time
of day.

Calligraphy

Calligraphy is the art of producing decorative writing, traditionally using a brush. It was introduced to Japan from China around the 4th century. Before then, the Japanese had no written language. At first, Chinese symbols, known as *kanji*, were used, but from the 9th century, the Japanese began to develop their own symbols, known as *kana*. In the 10th century many women writers used the more elegant *kana* script to write poetry and stories. By the **Edo period** people from all social classes were taught calligraphy.

Calligraphy is mostly done on paper or silk, but it also appears as decoration on objects such as **lacquer** boxes and pottery teapots. It is the brushwork that gives a piece of calligraphy its individual character and beauty: the lines can be thick or thin, smooth or rough, wet or dry, widely spaced or close together. Calligraphy is often done on decorated paper, which adds to the beauty of the finished work.

Modern calligraphy

In modern Japan, as in the rest of the world, people use pens and computers for everyday writing, but calligraphy is still a popular art form and an important part of the culture. There are examples of calligraphy in all aspects of modern Japanese life—for example, on the covers of books or magazines, on clothing and other textiles, and on restaurant signs. Many priests still make a good living from writing **Zen** sayings on scrolls to put on the walls of tea houses.

After World War II, a new style of calligraphy, called avant-garde, came into use. The symbols are based on the traditional scripts, but the artist alters them so that they look quite different—bolder and more dramatic. Sometimes they are changed so much that they can no longer be read as writing and instead become abstract pictures.

Calligraphy is taught in Japanese schools and is highly valued as a skill. Competitions are held every year, including contests in Chinese-style, Japanese-style, and avant-garde calligraphy.

Tools of the trade

The tools of a calligrapher are brushes, a stick of ink, and an inkstone. These are kept in a writing box called a *suzuribako*, together with a water dropper. You drip some water onto one end of the inkstone, grind some ink onto the other end, then mix the two until the ink is the right consistency. Calligraphy brushes are made from different types of animal hair. Some types absorb more ink than others, which produces different results. Traditionally, brushes were made from the hairs of wolves, squirrels, weasels, and badgers. Today the hairs are more likely to come from dogs, cats, deer, goats, or horses.

Poetic art

Many calligraphers use the words of poems as their text. Traditional Japanese poetry is written in verses of five lines, called *waka,* or three lines, called **haiku,** rather than in pairs of lines like most Chinese and Western poetry. In the early 17th century, the calligrapher Koetsu and the painter Sotatsu collaborated to create several works of art. Sotatsu painted gold and silver designs onto paper scrolls, then Koetsu added calligraphy of famous *waka* poems.

This design of cranes in flight is a typical example of the collaboration between the calligrapher Koetsu and the painter Sotatsu.

Theater

Theater has been an important art form in Japan since the 15th century. The two main types of Japanese drama are **Noh** and **Kabuki**. There are also puppet plays called **Bunraku**. All these, particularly Kabuki, are still popular forms of entertainment today.

Noh plays

Noh plays derived from the ancient religious dances that took place outside temples. They were first performed for the **noble** classes in the late 14th century at court and in temples.

Noh is a solemn and highly symbolic drama that uses ancient language and combines poetry, story, song, music, and dance. The words are chanted or sung and the actors move very little, using ritualized steps. The story line usually involves the main character reflecting on his or her life and seeking redemption for earlier wrongdoings. A Noh performance generally consists of three plays interspersed with two lighter comic interludes called *Kyogen*. These provide a contrast to the solemnity of the main story, and in *Kyogen* some parts are played by women. There are usually only two or three actors in a whole play, and all the parts in the main story are played by men.

Stage, music, props, and costumes

The traditional stage for a Noh play is a square wooden platform with a curved, tiled roof. There is no curtain and the only scenery is a **stylized** tree painted on the back wall. Actors get on and off the stage via a long, narrow walkway along the back. A group of musicians playing drums and flutes and another group of chanters sit on the stage throughout the performance.

The only props the actors use are folding fans, which can symbolize anything from a sword to a cup. Noh actors wear heavy, ornate silk costumes, often expensively decorated with gold thread.

Puppet theater

Puppet theater first appeared as a general form early in the 11th century, but the specialized form known as Bunraku developed in the 18th and 19th centuries. At one time, puppet plays were as popular as Kabuki plays, and the top puppet operators were celebrated as actors. All the puppets' voices are provided by a chanter, accompanied by a musician playing a stringed instrument called a **shamisen**.

Each major puppet is operated by three people who use sticks and internal springs and strings. Traditionally, the operators stood out of sight in a trench, two of them wearing black robes and hoods and the main operator often wearing brighter clothes and no hood. Today, all three operators are on the stage in full view of the audience. The main operator works the head and the right arm, another works the left arm, and the third works the legs. The puppets have movable eyelids, eyeballs, mouths, and eyebrows.

Puppets' bodies are made of wood and paper, and their heads are made of wood and painted with powdered sea shells. They have human hair and some wear colorful painted paper hats. Their costumes are made of silk or linen, which is often embroidered.

Masks

In Noh drama many of the actors wear wooden masks. The art of carving and painting masks is carried out by specialist sculptors and traditionally handed down from father to son. Making a mask takes weeks or even months. The features are carved with chisels, first roughly, and then more finely. The surface is smoothed with sandpaper; brass eyes and teeth are added; a base coat of white paint is applied, followed by six coats of skin-colored paint; and, finally, details of hair and eyes are painted on. The maker usually writes his name in gold on the back. There are standard types of masks representing more than 200 different characters, including a fisherman, a bewitching woman, a prince, and a range of gods and demons.

This Noh mask of a woman dates from the Momoyama period.

Kabuki theater

Kabuki theater began in the early 17th century, and during the **Edo period** it became one of the most popular forms of entertainment in towns and cities. The art of Kabuki grew alongside the *ukiyo-e* style of painting and was a great source of inspiration for many of the woodblock print designers. There are three main types of Kabuki plays: historical, domestic, and dance pieces. Most fans, though, go to the theater to see their favorite actors regardless of the play.

Kabuki makes use of features from ancient Japanese dances, from Noh plays, and from puppet theater. The themes come from epics and legends, and the plays are full of violence, heroic actions, dramatic effects, and conflicts of love and duty. Appealing to a more modern audience than the earlier Noh dramas, the Kabuki plays are more natural, though stylized gestures and movements are still used. Actors move more freely and use a more ordinary way of speaking. Today attempts are made to update plays and use exciting stage techniques to attract modern audiences.

An ornately costumed Kabuki actor strikes a dramatic pose in this scene from a contemporary performance.

The performance

The Kabuki stage has a curtain and a long passageway leading out to the auditorium, along which the actors run to make dramatic entrances and exits. For some performances, a revolving stage is used. The actors use a combination of dialogue and dance accompanied by drums, flutes, shamisen, and chanting. To add to the spectacle, special sound effects are made by striking together two wooden blocks that make a cracking noise. Kabuki actors wear magnificent silk costumes, with the exact style depending on the type of play.

The audience sits in rows of seats or in boxes at the sides of the theater. Kabuki is seen more as popular entertainment than as serious theater, and silence during a performance is not normally required. Prints from Edo times show the audience eating, drinking, and chatting while the play is going on, and this still happens today. Including intermissions, the average length of a performance is five hours.

Dressing up

In early Kabuki performances, both men and women acted. But in 1629 the **shogun** banned women from taking part. From then on, all female roles were played by men known as *onnagata*. To play women, male actors wore heavy makeup and wigs and, from the evidence of the color prints, they looked fairly convincing! They trained for many years to learn the art of female impersonation. In recent years there have been attempts to introduce female actors again, but these have failed.

Keep it in the family

Each role from the Kabuki plays is allocated to a particular family of actors that has played that role from generation to generation. The most famous family was, and still is, the Danjuro family. They play the hero who puts wrongs right and is applauded every time he appears. He wears a bright red **kimono** patterned with three white squares. Today, the National Theater in Tokyo trains young Kabuki actors who are not from the traditional families.

Makeup

First, an actor puts wax on his eyebrows and oil on his face to help the makeup stick. Then he covers his face with a base of very thick white cream called *oshiroi*. The shade of white depends on the role he is playing, such as whether he should appear young or old, a prince or a commoner. He then paints lines around his eyes and mouth to accentuate them and draws on a new pair of eyebrows.

A Kabuki actor applies stage makeup prior to a performance.

47

Cross-Currents

The currents of influence from other cultures have naturally had a bearing on the development of Japanese art. Currents travel in the opposite direction, too, with Japanese art forms influencing the art of other cultures. These cross-currents are more apparent at some times in history than others.

From the 6th century on, Japanese art was influenced by the arts of its near neighbors, China and Korea, where techniques were more advanced. Travel between the countries was common, and landscape painting, porcelain, and **calligraphy** are just a few of the art forms that arrived from China. Many techniques in pottery were introduced by Korean **immigrants** living in Japan, and their rough wares had great influence on **tea ceremony** pottery. Also, **Buddhism,** which was the inspiration for virtually all Japanese art for several hundred years, came from China via Korea.

Chinese or Japanese?

During the **Muromachi period,** monk painters such as Sesshu (*see page 11*) were inspired by the ink landscapes of steep mountains and gnarled trees created by Chinese painters. The Chinese influence on Sesshu's work is clear, but there are differences: The composition of the Japanese landscapes is less formally structured, the mountains and trees are more sketchy, and there is more empty space. In other words, the paintings have been made more Japanese.

Detail from *Clear Weather in the Valley*, a 13th-century Chinese landscape painting.

Japan welcomed new art forms, initially imitating them but then adapting them to a more Japanese style. For example, techniques for making ornate Chinese porcelain were used. However, instead of making regularly shaped plates in sets of equal numbers as the Chinese did, Japanese potters developed all kinds of new shapes and produced them in sets of three or five instead—an example of the Japanese liking for **asymmetry.**

As Japanese art forms took on their own identity, some began to influence Chinese art. For example, Japanese painted screens were **exported** to both China and Korea, and Chinese potters copied Japanese *Imari* porcelain to make ceramics known as Chinese *Imari.* In the 20th century, many Chinese and Korean painters came to study at Japanese art schools.

Western influence

Japan has been influenced by Western culture at various points in its history. Although the country was closed to the outside world during the **Edo period,** the Dutch had a trading post at Nagasaki in southern Japan. Via this route Western art forms entered Japan and had some influence on art styles. At the end of the Edo period, when Japan opened its doors to the West, European and North American experts were brought in to set up art schools and Japanese students were sent abroad to study art.

After World War II, Western influences poured into Japan and affected many of its art forms. This is a process that continues to some extent today. Garden designers make use of Western features such as lawns, many **Kabuki** actors also star in television soap operas, and architects design Western-style buildings. At times, Japanese art has seemed in danger of losing its own cultural identity. That identity has survived, though, and in today's international world, traditional and Western art styles exist side by side, complementing each other.

Tokyo City Hall was designed by Tange Kenzo, the internationally renowned Japanese architect. The building, completed in 1991, is the tallest in Tokyo.

Architecture

At the end of the Edo period, Western building techniques using stone and brick were introduced throughout Japan. After much research into earthquake-proof construction methods, reinforced concrete (later with a steel frame) took over as the most popular building material. During the second half of the 20th century, the design of Western-style buildings became a recognized art form. A number of buildings are internationally renowned, and many Japanese architects design buildings in other countries, too. Western architects, such as the American Frank Lloyd Wright, have been influenced by the creations of their Japanese counterparts, attaching importance to features such as open space, clean lines, natural light, and the link between indoors and outdoors.

49

The influence of prints

Woodblock prints have probably had more influence on the Western world than any other Japanese art form. When they were introduced to Europe and the United States in the 19th century, they were instantly popular and had enormous impact on the work of the **Impressionist** and **Post-Impressionist** artists.

The works of the Impressionists were radically different from contemporary European painting styles. The painters revealed their debt to the Japanese print designers in several ways. They took as their subject matter colorful landscapes, beautiful women, and scenes from everyday life, including the world of entertainment, much like the *ukiyo-e* artists. Impressionist compositions were often asymmetrical—in other words, the main subject or subjects might be anywhere in the painting, not necessarily in the center. As their name suggests, the aim of the Impressionists was to give an impression of the subject rather than to produce a realistic copy. This was another trait shared with Japanese art.

European admirers

The list of European painters who admired and were inspired by Japanese prints includes the French artists Claude Monet, Edgar Degas, Paul Gauguin, and Henri de Toulouse-Lautrec, and the Dutch artist Vincent van Gogh. The print artists who influenced them included Hokusai, Hiroshige, and Utamaro. Both Monet and van Gogh collected Japanese landscape prints, and van Gogh made copies of several of Hiroshige's works. His use of strong outlines, bright colors, and dynamic design owes much to the Japanese prints.

Two Women at Arles by Vincent van Gogh (1888).

This still from the film *Pokemon* shows the bright colors and black lines typical in modern Japanese *manga*.

Just plain pottery

The British potter Bernard Leach was born in Hong Kong in 1887 and studied in Japan from 1911 until 1919. On later visits to Japan, he worked with folk potters who were making pottery in the traditional plain "tea-wares" style. He also befriended Dr. Soetsu Yanagi and Shoji Hamada. When Leach set up his own pottery studio in St. Ives, Cornwall, in Great Britain, he began to make earthenware and stoneware pots, imitating the simple styles he had seen in Japan. His pots, often asymmetrical and undecorated, had great appeal and he played an important role in teaching the Western world to appreciate handmade pottery as an art form.

East and West, old and new

As we have seen in this book, many of Japan's traditional art forms are still thriving today. They are changing, adapting to the modern world, and taking on Western influences, but there is still great respect and admiration for the traditions of the past among both young and old people. The West continues to be influenced by things Japanese: **Minimalism** has been taken to extremes in art and design, and in recent years garden design, **interior design**, computer games, and restaurants have all been inspired by Japan.

One current example of this influence on Western art forms is the genre of Japanese comics, cartoons, and animated films called *manga*. The animations are often called *anime*. Many types of *manga* have features in common with Western cartoons and comics, and some *manga* writers have been influenced by, for example, Walt Disney. Still, the simple lines and **stylized** features are distinctly Japanese. Indeed, the humorous ink drawings of animals in the 12th century *Scroll of the Frolicking Animals* (see page 10) bear a striking resemblance to modern *manga*, illustrating how Japanese cartoons have been an art form for a very long time.

Further Resources

Further reading

Addiss, Stephen. *How to Look at Japanese Art.* New York: Harry N. Abrams, Inc., Publishers, 1996.

Dorling Kindersley Publishing Staff. *Eyewitness Travel Guide to Japan.* New York: Dorling Kindersley, 2003.

Finley, Carol. *Art of Japan: Wood Block Color Prints.* Minneapolis: Lerner, 1998.

Hammond, Paula. *Culture and Costumes of China and Japan.* Broomall, Penn.: Mason Crest, 2002.

Stevens, Clive. *Step by Step: Origami.* Chicago: Heinemann Library, 2002.

In general, guide books to Japan often have good sections on Japanese culture.

Websites

www.fix.co.jp/kabuki/sound.htbBroml
Listen to different Kabuki instruments and hear fans shouting support for their favorite actors.

www.japaneseculture.about.com/
Links to many websites on all aspects of Japanese art.

www.japaneseart.org
Excellent resource for information on and links about Japanese art.

www.jinjapan.org/museum
Good general introduction to different aspects of Japanese arts.

www.paperfolding.com
Information about origami and lots of step-by-step examples of things to make.

www.sas.upenn.edu/~amorentz/index.htm
Excellent examples of Noh masks.

Places to visit

United States

Allen Memorial Art Museum (AMAN), Oberlin, Ohio

Arthur M. Sackler Museum, Cambridge, Massachusetts

Asian Art Museum, San Francisco

Brooklyn Museum of Art (BMA), Brooklyn, New York

Cleveland Museum of Art

Dayton Art Institute, Dayton, Ohio

Denver Art Museum

Honolulu Academy of Arts

Indianapolis Museum of Art

Johnson Museum of Art, Ithaca, New York

Kimbell Art Museum, Fort Worth, Texas

Los Angeles County Museum of Art (LACMA)

Metropolitan Museum of Art, New York

Minneapolis Institute of Art

Pacific Asia Museum, Los Robles, California

Peabody Essex Museum, Salem, Massachusetts

Philadelphia Museum of Art

Phoenix Art Museum

Portland Art Museum

San Diego Museum of Art

Seattle Asian Art Museum

Wright Museum House, Beloit, Wisconsin

Canada

Art Gallery of Greater Victoria

Royal Ontario Museum, Toronto

Glossary

Asuka period years in Japanese history from 552 to 646 C.E.

asymmetry lack of equality or balance

Buddhism religion introduced to Japan from China in the 6th century

Bunraku type of Japanese drama involving the use of ornate puppets

calligraphy art of producing decorative writing, traditionally with a brush

Edo period years in Japanese history from 1603 to 1868 C.E.

emperor powerful ruler

export to send goods to another country for sale

falconer person who keeps, trains, or hunts with falcons, hawks, or other birds of prey

haiku three-lined Japanese poem of seventeen syllables, traditionally taking the natural world as its subject matter

Hakuho period years in Japanese history from 646 to 710 C.E.

Heian period years in Japanese history from 794 to 1185 C.E.

hilt handle of a weapon or tool

immigrant person who comes to live permanently in a foreign country

Impressionists group of French painters from the second half of the 19th century who aimed to produce an impression of a subject, rather than a realistic representation. They often painted landscapes.

insulator thing or substance through which heat does not easily pass

interior design art or process of designing the internal decoration of a room or building

Jomon period years in Japanese history from around 10,500 B.C.E. to 300 B.C.E.

Kabuki type of Japanese drama that began in the early 17th century

Kamakura period years in Japanese history from 1185 to 1333 C.E.

kimono traditional Japanese long, loose robe, with wide sleeves that is tied with a sash

Kofun period years in Japanese history from around 300 to 552 C.E.

lacquer hard, waterproof substance that comes from the sap of the lacquer tree, used to cover wood and other materials

mass production production of large quantities of an item, usually by machine

minimalism originally an art style that used simple and often large forms. Today also used in many forms of design, for example interior design, to produce a simple, uncluttered look.

Momoyama period years in Japanese history from 1573 to 1603 C.E.

Muromachi period years in Japanese history from 1333 to 1573 C.E.

Nara period years in Japanese history from 710 to 794 C.E.

narrative concerned with telling or showing a story

netsuke   small carved toggle used to hang things from the sash of a kimono

noble   person belonging to the highest class of society

Noh   type of Japanese drama that began in the late 14th century

pagoda   Buddhist holy building, usually a tower with several tiers

plate boundary   joint between two large areas of the Earth's crust. Moving plates create friction, which can result in earthquakes and volcanoes.

Post-Impressionists   group of artists, including van Gogh and Gauguin, who built upon the style of the Impressionists and explored color, line, form, and the emotional response of the artist

Pure Land   form of Buddhism in which followers worship the Buddha Amitabha and aim for rebirth in the Western Paradise (the "Pure Land") by faithfully invoking Amitabha's name

relief   form of design in which the figure is raised from or higher than its background

samurai   Japanese warrior class set up in the Kamakura period and abolished at the end of the Edo period

scabbard   cover for the blade of a sword or dagger

shamisen   Japanese three-stringed musical instrument, similar to a lute

Shinto   Japanese religion dating from the 8th century and based on the worship of nature and one's ancestors

shogun   Japanese military chief who usually had more actual power than the emperor (Kamakura period to end of Edo period)

shrine   holy place usually marked by a building

stylized   shown in a symbolic, unrealistic style

tatami mat   traditional Japanese floor covering made of a rectangular rush-covered straw mat

tea ceremony   traditional Japanese ritual of serving and drinking tea

Yayoi period   years in Japanese history from 300 B.C.E. to 300 C.E.

Zen   form of Buddhism introduced to Japan in the 12th century that became very influential there. The emphasis is on meditation and intuition, rather than ritual worship and the study of religious texts.

Index

j709.52   Khanduri, Kamini.
KHA
           Japanese art &
           culture.

Wallingford Public Library
Wallingford, CT 06492

A2170 503868 9

CHILDREN'S LIBRARY

WALLINGFORD PUBLIC LIBRARY
200 NO MAIN ST
WALLINGFORD CT 06492

BAKER & TAYLOR